You've Got This

FOR TEENS

Copyright © 2019

All rights reserved. This book or any portion thereof may not be reproduced or used in any manner whatsoever without the express written permission of the author except for the use of brief quotations in a book review.

Printed in Australia

First Printing, 2019

ISBN: 978-0-6484641-9-8

White Light Publishing

Melton, VIC, Australia 3337

whitelightpublishing.com.au

It's not easy being a teenager. You aren't allowed to behave like a child, but you still aren't given the freedoms of an adult. You're in transition and it can be awfully overwhelming sometimes. You've probably heard this a million times before, but trust me when I say that things *do* become clearer. You will find yourself, and know where you fit into this big, wide world.

Life is full of lessons. This part of your life is one big whirlwind where things can very easily get on top of you, and time passes by in a flash. I hope that the words inside this book help to remind you that you ARE acknowledged, you ARE understood, and there is ALWAYS support around you — whether you're aware of it or not.

Most importantly, I want you to know that you're not meant to have life all figured out yet, so give yourself a break and allow yourself to just be YOU.

You've got this.

I am not my parents. Their past does not define my future.

I can change my mind without the need to explain why.

It is safe for me to be powerful.

My opinions are important.

It's a sign of strength to ask for help when I need it.

There's no such thing as a mistake. It's merely a lesson I've learnt.

Time to get serious. What should really be my priority right now?

I am ME, and that is more than enough.

I have a voice and it should be heard.

I am deserving of respect as much as anyone else.

What is it that you'd really like to be doing? What small action can you take now to get the ball rolling?

My appearance does not define who I am.

It is my right to explore my passions, regardless of what others may think.

It's perfectly okay not to have all the answers.

(No one does)

If my gut is telling me something doesn't feel right, I'll trust it. Every single time.

My true strengths are not something to keep hidden away. It's time for me to show them to the world.

Which difficult conversation have you been putting off having?

(It may feel uncomfortable, but you know it needs to happen sooner or later.)

It's healthy for me to open up and be vulnerable.

I don't rely on others to make me feel important.

Others' issues are not my own. I can be a support, yes, but I do not need to take on their issues.

I can say yes.

What are three things you're grateful for right now?

You know in your heart who will listen without judgement. Reach out to them and talk it out.

(You'll feel so much better afterward)

Never, ever underestimate the power of being you.

It's okay for me to have a break and do absolutely nothing every now and then.

If I want it badly enough,
I can make it happen.

Is this a 'make or break' moment, or just a hurdle?

(Coz remember, you've got this)

A real friend will tell you the truth — even when you don't want to hear it.

Are you seeing the situation from all angles? Try and look at it from another's perspective.

(It may just give you the insight you need)

It's okay for me to honestly say, "I don't know".

You're not supposed to have it all figured out yet. You have all the time in the world.

Own who you are. Every single part of you.

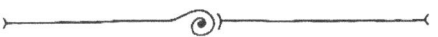

Sometimes, it's better to just walk away.

No matter what anyone says, it IS possible for males and females to just be friends, and great ones at that!

It's okay to feel sad sometimes — it means I'm human.

Even though I risk looking like a fool, would I rather miss out on the opportunity?

It's my absolute right to always feel safe in any situation. If I don't, then I need to speak up.

Remember to act silly sometimes. Be weird and own it.

Look in the mirror. There is no one like you. No one. And that is incredible.

There is always, always someone who will understand — no matter what it is.

I can say no.

Ask yourself, "Is this really worth my energy?"

Who in your life just 'gets' you? Have you ever told them that?

In times of stress, I know that if I focus on just one thing at a time, I will make things much easier on myself.

What is it that YOU

want?

I know that taking care of my body is good for my mental health too.

(And yep, that includes getting enough sleep!)

I do not need to be strong
all the time.

Never underestimate the inner turmoil within the bully. There's always more to their story than you know.

You aren't expected to be an expert in everything. Nobody is. Your strengths are yours alone, and that's enough.

I've got this.

Why would you want to be the same as everyone else anyway? You're awesome in your own right.

(Yes, you are)

It's perfectly healthy for me to feel angry, so long as I express it without intentionally harming others.

No matter how overwhelming life may feel right now, it will pass.

I will be heard.

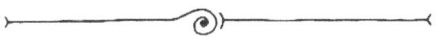

I don't need to make the same choices my friends make. I am my own person.

Reach out to a friend today — just for a chat. You never know how much they might need it.

The people who truly love me will always understand,

(no matter how crazy I might sound)

It's healthy for me to cry
when I feel I need to

(and I know I'll always feel better
afterward)

Anger. Disappointment. Sadness. They're all real feelings, and I'm allowed to express them.

Think about the last challenge you had. How much have you learnt from the experience?

I CAN figure this out.

Here's something to think about... Are you 'bullying' yourself?

(be mindful of your self-talk)

Stop for a moment. Now take three deep breaths.

(Ahhhh...)

Have you got too much going on right now? Maybe it's time for a break.

Step out of your comfort zone — just a little. Try something new.

———⊚)———

Name at least three things you love about yourself. Go!

Is there a chance you're overthinking the situation?

Before reacting, take a step back and look at the situation again. (Calmly)

What do you value? Do you surround yourself with people who hold similar values?

I have the power to control my thoughts.

It's perfectly natural for me to feel confused sometimes. I can come back to it when my head feels clearer.

It's time to get creative.
What can you do today to
allow your creativity to
flow?

―――――⊚―――――

Whether you believe it or not, you are loved. Just as you are.

I am true to myself, even when it's not received well.

What I feel is important, and I have the right to express those feelings.

How can you be compassionate towards someone today?

I can admit when I'm wrong.

We're all human. Remember that.

I am appreciated for who I am.

I don't get caught up in gossip and bitchiness. I'm way better than that.

My Affirmations

Use the following pages to add your own affirmations, words of inspiration, or notes to remind yourself of who you are and what's important to you.

It's ALWAYS okay to ask for help.

(always)

You should never, ever feel as though you're on this journey alone. If you don't feel as though you can talk to anyone around you, please reach out to one of the organisations on the following page. Alternatively, I am always here to lend a listening ear.

You can contact me on Facebook or Instagram, or via email at whitelightpublishinghouse@outlook.com.

Much love, Christie

Lifeline – for all ages

CALL: 13 11 14 (Available 24/7)

Visit: lifeline.org.au

Kids Helpline – For ages 5 – 25

CALL: 1800 55 1800 (Available 24/7)

Visit: kidshelpline.com.au

Suicide Call Back Service – For ages 15+

CALL: 1300 659 467 (Available 24/7)

Visit: suicidecallbackservice.org.au

1800 RESPECT – All ages

CALL: 1800 737 732

Visit: 1800respect.org.au

Headspace — For ages 12 – 25

CALL: 1800 650 890 (9am – 1am)

Visit: headspace.org.au

ReachOut — For ages 18 – 25

Visit: au.reachout.com

SANE

CALL: 1800 187 263

Visit: sane.org

ConnectED Space

Visit: connectedspace.com.au

Visit our online shop:

www.whitelightshop.com

www.ingramcontent.com/pod-product-compliance
Lightning Source LLC
Chambersburg PA
CBHW072058290426
44110CB00014B/1733